THE HEART:
HIS WORDS + MY THOUGHTS

DEVOTIONS BY

TANYA SWYGERT

WESTBOW
PRESS®
A DIVISION OF THOMAS NELSON
& ZONDERVAN

Unless otherwise indicated, all scriptures are taken from the King James Version of the Bible.

Any Hebrew or Greek definitions of scriptural words are taken from The New Strong's Expanded Exhaustive Concordance of the Bible by James Strong, L.L.D., S.T.D. (2010)

This book is a work of non-fiction. Unless otherwise noted, the author and the publisher make no explicit guarantees as to the accuracy of the information contained in this book and in some cases, names of people and places have been altered to protect their privacy.

WestBow Press books may be ordered through booksellers or by contacting:

WestBow Press
A Division of Thomas Nelson & Zondervan
1663 Liberty Drive
Bloomington, IN 47403
www.westbowpress.com
1 (866) 928-1240

ISBN: 978-1-9736-1005-2 (sc)
ISBN: 978-1-9736-1006-9 (e)

Library of Congress Control Number: 2017918191

Print information available on the last page.

WestBow Press rev. date: 11/29/2017

Dedication

I dedicate this book to:

My Lord and Savior, Jesus Christ, because he makes all things possible!

My husband and three children who occupy so many of my personal heart thoughts!

My extended family members and dear friends, who encouraged me along the way!

I love you all!

Tanya

Contents

Keep Your Heart with All Diligence

> Keep your heart with all diligence;
> for out of it are the issues of life.
>
> —Proverbs 4:23

Several years ago, I was asked to give an inspirational message for our small church assembly. As I meditated on God's Word and prayed for direction on what the Lord would have me share, this thought came to me: "Keep your heart with all diligence; for out of it are the issues of life" (Proverbs 4:23). In studying my *Strong's Concordance* for the Hebrew meanings of the words in this scripture, I found it interesting that the word *keep* (5341) means "to guard, protect, or maintain," and the word *diligence* (4929) had the connotation of placing a man on post to guard, such as a prison guard monitoring every encounter. What further caught my attention was the definition for the word *issues* (3444), which implies that the heart is the exit point or the source of departure for the course our lives will take.

I am very visual, and various images came to mind that helped symbolize Proverbs 4:23. With my spiritual eye, I understood more clearly one of the roles the Holy Spirit fulfills in our lives. Imagine with me the Holy Spirit standing guard to prevent the enemy from entering areas of our hearts despite numerous attempts. The Holy Spirit is that guard that abides forever (John 16:8–13). If we allow the Holy Spirit to lead and guide us, we will have fewer issues with the evil thoughts, adulteries, fornications, murders, thefts, covetousness, wickedness, deceit, lasciviousness, evil eyes, blasphemy, pride, and foolishness that can proceed from our hearts (Mark 7:21–22)

Multiple scriptures help us see why it is so critical that we guard our hearts. In Genesis 6:5, the scriptures record that "God saw that the wickedness of man was great in the Earth, and that every imagination of the thoughts of his heart was only evil continually." This observation of humanity's heart grieved the Lord and provoked him to wipe humankind from the face of the earth (Genesis 6:7). After the flood, the scriptures note that "the Lord said in his heart, I will not again curse the ground any more for man's sake; for the imagination of man's heart is evil from his youth" (Genesis 8:21). It's scary to think that even from our youth, the thoughts of our hearts are continually evil! With all these maladies, it is no wonder the Word exhorts us to guard our hearts.

Reflecting on these scriptures, I began to realize how many times I had failed to heed the warning to guard my heart, and I felt as if my heart had been penetrated by one of those fiery darts of the wicked (Ephesians 6:16). Unfortunately, there are too many testimonies from others that confirm that I was not Satan's only target for this type of attack. If it were not for the grace of God, I am sure these reflections would discourage me and cause me to feel that there was no hope for me. I thank God for his mercies and compassions that never fail (Lamentations 3:23), and I appreciate the promise that "if we confess our sins, he is faithful and just to forgive us our sins, and to cleanse us from all unrighteousness" (1 John 1:9).

Since delivering that first message about guarding the heart, I have revisited Proverbs 4:23 on many occasions. Further studies on the heart continue to remind me of how critical the command is, because the Word of God indicates that our hearts can be obstinate (Deuteronomy 2:30), pained (Psalm 55:4), proud (Proverbs 28:25), fearful (Isaiah 35:4), rebellious (Jeremiah 5:23), foolish (Romans 1:21), and blinded (Ephesians 4:18). I'm encouraged by the challenge to guard my heart because I also know that our hearts can be clean (Psalm 51:10), fixed (Psalm 57:7), and pure (Matthew 5:8). If we can master the task of guarding our hearts (and by God's grace and mercy, we can), we have the assurance that Christ will dwell in our hearts by faith (Ephesians 3:17). This would also help us know that the course of life we take would be pleasing in God's sight. What a comforting thought!

Thy Word Have I Hid in Mine Heart

Thy word have I hid in mine heart, that
I might not sin against thee.

—Psalm 119:11

Psalm 119, the longest chapter in the Bible, is an acrostic poem in praise of the scriptures. Each stanza has eight verses and is identified by the twenty-two letters in the Hebrew alphabet. Tradition suggests that King David used this poem to teach Solomon the letters in the Hebrew alphabet. Some suggest that this was David's way of sharing the importance of God's law as a roadmap for successful living. Regardless of the purpose, it is interesting to note that the word *heart* is used fifteen different times.

When I prepare for a Bible study, I constantly consult *Strong's Exhaustive Concordance of the Bible*. Over the years,

I have found it to be an invaluable resource. According to *Strong's*, the primary Hebrew word for *heart* in Psalm 119 is *labe* (3820), which has a figurative use suggesting that the word *heart* is synonymous with our feelings, our will, and even our intellect. It can also be said that the heart is the center for anything. This meaning was used fourteen times in Psalm 119. The other meaning for the word *heart* used in this psalm (v. 7) is *labab*, and this refers to the heart as the most interior organ.

By now, you may be asking why I have just given you this vocabulary lesson. Blame it on the educator in me, but I just feel that it is critical to fully understand what we are reading. In verse 2 of Psalm 119, the psalmist lays the foundation early that a blessed (happy) life is given to those who keep God's testimonies and seek him with their whole hearts. This suggests to me that I must pursue God with all my feelings, emotions, will, and intellect. In short, it's everything that I am feeling or thinking. Several verses in Psalm 119 (vv. 2, 10, 34, 58, 69, and 145) use the expression "whole heart," which means all of it!

Psalm 119 emphasizes the magnitude of God's Word. God's Word is his law, his testimonies, his ways, his precepts, his statutes, his commandments, and his judgments! In verse Psalm 119:11, the writer declares, "Thy (God's) word have I hid in mine heart, that I might not sin against thee (God)." More modern language views it as banking God's promises in a vault of our hearts so that we do not allow sin to bankrupt us. Another analogy is viewing God's Word as treasure that is hidden. Perhaps if we remained conscious of the fact that our sins are sins against God Almighty, we would allow the Word to check us before we yielded to life's temptations. Very few of us have Joseph's integrity when he refused Potiphar's wife (Genesis 39:9). Joseph questioned her and asked, "How can I do this great wickedness, and sin against God?" What would the historical outcome have been if David had taken Joseph's attitude when he committed adultery with Bathsheba, wife of Uriah (2 Samuel 11)? Since none of us were there, we can't say what transpired in David's heart before he became spiritually bankrupt. Perhaps it was too many withdrawals from the bank of God's Word and not enough spiritual deposits. How is it that we can understand it so well in the natural world that we can't draw out more than we put in, but we fail to see the spiritual implications? If we want God's blessings, we must take the time to hide God's Word in our hearts. It is labor-intensive but well worth the effort!

Trust in the Lord with All Thine Heart

Trust in the Lord with all thine heart; and
lean not unto thine own understanding.

—Proverbs 3:5

"Trust in the Lord with all thine heart" is a familiar scripture to many people. However, just because it is familiar doesn't make it easy to do! In this scripture, the word *trust* means "to quickly go for shelter or protection from danger or distress." If I were to rewrite this scripture, it might read like this: "Whenever you find yourself in a dangerous or distressful situation, quickly go to Jesus for shelter so that he can hide you and keep you safe!" I would further add, "While going to him, your every thought, intent, and feeling should be focused solely on him." To do this, we must have complete confidence in

Jesus Christ. And we are only able to do this if we have built relationships with him and realized that his words are faithful and true.

In my counseling and school psychology courses that I took several years ago, we were required to study various theories on psychosocial development. We were taught about how important the first few years of life were to our overall development. I was always fascinated by the belief that developing trust in the first two years of life was a critical factor in developing relationships. Experiences that left babies with feelings of insecurity during their formative years could contribute to their mistrust of others as they got older.

Satan knows the importance of trust in relationships, and that is why he continuously attempts to poison our minds regarding God's Word. As humans, we are limited by our five senses, and we often only respond to what we can see, hear, smell, taste, and touch. Because God is a spirit, we can't always determine how he is operating in our lives. This is why the second part of Proverbs 3:5 is so critical. God's Word implores us to "lean not unto our own understanding." While every word from God is "quick and powerful" (Hebrews 4:12), Isaiah 55:9 puts us in check by reminding us that "God's thoughts are not our thoughts, and our ways are not His ways." If you are like me, at one time or another, Satan has used this device against you to defeat you and rob you of God's purpose for your life!

As with other aspects of life, I firmly believe that the theory of how people develop trust in others and their environment is analogous to our beginning relationship with Jesus Christ. I have met many people who had difficulty trusting Jesus's love for them because of their inability to trust people in their lives. It's hard to develop a trusting relationship with Jesus if we don't read God's Word and study to show ourselves approved unto him (2 Timothy 2:15). As we study, this scripture also commands us to "rightly divide the word." If we have misunderstandings about God's promises, we will become mistrustful because we were expecting something that God never promised.

Praying to God is also essential if we are to develop a trusting relationship with Jesus Christ. In 1 Thessalonians 5:17, we are encouraged to "pray without ceasing." When we read Philippians 4:6–7, we see that we shouldn't be concerned for anything because we are to pray and ask with thanksgiving. If we do this, then we will have the peace of God that passes all understanding. God promises to keep our heart through Christ Jesus.

The Heart is Deceitful

The heart is deceitful above all things and
desperately wicked: who can know it?

—Jeremiah 17:9

I will be the first to admit that I love romantic movies. Sadly, I confess that I could watch a marathon of sappy movies and be quite content. I don't need company while enjoying the predictableness of girl-meets-boy. Then drama pursues, only to have it end up that the girl walks happily down the aisle. Yes, I believe in love, or the illusion of love! This thought brings me to the scripture that is the subject of this lesson. If the scripture in Jeremiah 17:9 declares that the heart is deceitful above all things and desperately wicked, how can any of us be certain that we are truly in love when we say we are? Even the prophet Jeremiah penned the question at the end of this verse (Jeremiah 17:9), "Who can know it?" Many modern song and movie titles paint a portrait of situations that began as love but ended as hate. It never ceases to amaze me when, in those movies, the confessions of love are quickly abandoned and replaced with a hate that is just as passionate.

According to King Solomon, there is "no new thing under the sun" (Ecclesiastes 1:9). Therefore, we can infer that there is a biblical reference about love going awry. In my opinion, one of the saddest is the story of David's son Amnon and how he declared that he was so in love with his half-sister, Tamar, that he made himself sick thinking of how he had to have her (2 Samuel 13:1–2). Of course, as Satan would have it, Amnon's best friend (who was also his first cousin) concocted a scheme to deceive Tamar into putting herself in a precarious situation, and she was raped by her brother Amnon (2 Samuel 13:3–14).

If Hollywood has scripted a movie using this biblical story, I have yet to see it. And, if this movie exists, I doubt it could do an adequate job in portraying Tamar's despair as she pleas with her brother not to make the situation worse by discarding her as a piece of trash that he has no more use for (2 Samuel 13:16-17). I have read this passage of scripture on several occasions, and each time, the impact on me has been the same! My heart aches for Tamar as she begins her walk of shame after she is thrown out of her brother's house (2 Samuel 13:17-19).

It may be blatant literary license on my part, but I can only imagine that the prophet Jeremiah must have been reflecting on Amnon's actions when he penned Jeremiah 17:9. According to 2 Samuel 13:15, after fulfilling his lustful desires, Amnon hated Tamar exceedingly: so, that the hatred wherewith he hated her was greater than the love wherewith he had loved her. After reading this, I want to ask Amnon, "I thought you said you loved her?"

Unfortunately, people like Amnon still exist today, and it is not gender or culturally specific. Our world is filled with countless stories of people being deceived by someone they thought loved them, only to find out they were being used to fulfill some vile desire. In many cases, it's not even sexual. Regardless of the circumstances, we still see that the heart is deceitful and can be desperately wicked, and only God can truly know it (1 Kings 8:39).

My Heart is Fixed, O God

My heart is fixed, O God, my heart is
fixed: I will sing and give praise.

—Psalm 57:7

I woke up one morning with these words on my heart:
"My heart is fixed, O God." As I researched these scriptures,
I discovered that David penned these words during one
of the times he was hiding from King Saul. In my opinion,
King David is one of the most interesting people in the
Bible, and time is limited to discuss the many aspects of
his life. What I like about David was his hope and trust in
God and his passion for the things of God. To describe
David's life as *complicated* would be an understatement.
I am sure that his biography would rival any of the reality
shows that are so popular in television today. Just think
about the many roles he played: youthful warrior, town

hero, hated rival, famous adulterer, conspirator, murderer, conqueror, beloved king, psalmist, and ancestor of Jesus Christ! What a script for a creative writer!

However, David is also described as a "man after God's own heart" (Acts 13:22). This suggests that David loved what God loved. We know that David was a worshipper and praised God (2 Samuel 6:14), for the scripture declares that when he was transporting the ark (the correct way), he danced before the Lord with all his might. In 2 Samuel, chapter 22, David is rendering a psalm of thanksgiving as he acknowledges the Lord for delivering him out of the hands of all his enemies, particularly from the hand of Saul. Several psalms are attributed to David and are filled with his adulation of God and his many wondrous works (examples: Psalms 3, 4, 5, 8, 9, 12-32, 35, 37, and 39).

Reading Psalm 57 took on new meaning for me as I considered how David must have felt as he fled from Saul. Think about it! David's zeal for God and his outrage over Goliath's audacity to defy the God of Israel is what brought David into Saul's awareness in the first place (1 Samuel 17:26). Truly, David had done Saul a great favor by destroying his enemy. Despite this, what was David's reward? To be hated because Saul was disobedient to God and suffered from a spirit of jealousy because of his self-esteem issues (1 Samuel 18: 8–9)?

Although I know how it feels to be betrayed by

someone who you thought was a friend, I can't remember being chased by someone to whom I was a loyal servant. There is no scripture to suggest that David directly did anything to personally harm Saul. In fact, the scriptures are explicit in that David did everything to revere Saul as king and never took advantage of opportunities to defend himself against Saul (1 Samuel 24). Despite this, in Psalm 57, David found himself hiding in a cave. I can only imagine what he was thinking. Through it all, David declared that his heart was fixed. In other words, no matter what David was experiencing, his heart was settled (steadfast) that God was going to deliver him. What a testimony!

The apostle Paul wrote that we are "troubled on every side, perplexed and persecuted" (2 Corinthians 4:8–9). However, praise be unto God, that's not the end of the story. When our hearts are fixed, we also know that we are not distressed, not in despair, not forsaken, and not destroyed (2 Corinthians 4:8–9). David's life is truly our example that God can deliver us regardless of the tactics or people Satan tries to use against us (Isaiah 54:17).

Let Not Your Heart
be Troubled

Let not your heart be troubled: ye
believe in God, believe also in me.

—John 14:1

Peace I leave with you, my peace I give unto you:
not as the world giveth, give I unto you. Let not
your heart be troubled, neither let it be afraid.

—John 14:27

While these words spoken by Jesus are powerful in
themselves, they seem to increase in magnitude when
read along with the verses in John, chapter 13. At least
they do to me! Let me explain my reasoning for this. The
verses in John 13 describe Jesus's actions as he has his

last Passover feast with his disciples, and there is a lot of detail packed in this chapter.

The tone for the chapter is set as the scripture reveals that Jesus is aware that his earthly ministry is near completion and that he has "loved his own which were in the world unto the very end" (John 13:1). Verse 2 describes how the devil put into Judas Iscariot's heart to betray Jesus (after the supper was ended). The next few verses detail how Jesus began to wash the disciples' feet and Peter's apparent astonishment at the Lord's actions. When Jesus explains that Simon Peter can have no part of him unless he does, Simon Peter goes overboard and declares, "Not my feet only, but also my hands and my head" (John 13:9). Although Simon Peter seems to miss the intent of Jesus's message, our Lord and Savior continues with his task and then takes an advantage of a teachable moment to instruct the disciples of what being a servant and a leader truly means.

After this instructional discourse, Jesus then informs the disciples that one of them would betray him (John 13:21), and the more vocal Simon Peter inquires who it will be (John 13:25). Jesus answered, "He it is to whom I shall give a sop, when I have dipped it" (John 13:26). Jesus does not publicly identify Judas, and Judas is able to depart into the night without the others actually knowing what is going on (John 13:28–30). After Judas departs, Jesus tells the disciples that now is the time for the Son to be glorified and for God to be glorified in him (John 13:31). He further tells the disciples that the true test of discipleship would be by the love they show to others (John 13:34–35).

I suppose at this point, Peter had heard all that he wanted to hear and asked Jesus where he was going (John 13:36). To this, Jesus replied, "Where he went, Peter couldn't follow him then, but would follow him later" (John 13:36). Apparently, Peter was not accepting of this idea and then declared that "he would lay down his life for Jesus's sake" (John 13:37). In his directness, Jesus countered Peter's proclamation with these words: "Will you lay down your life for my sake? Surely, surely, I say unto thee, the cock shall not crow, until you have denied me three times" (John 13:38).

It is after these words of prophetic betrayal that Jesus then tells them, "Let not your heart be troubled." How could you not be troubled at such declarations! Nevertheless, Jesus is trying to let his disciples know that there is no reason to get agitated or riled up because of what they may do or what might happen to them. This message applies to us today. If we believe in (trust) God, then we should also believe in (trust) Jesus. John 14 is Jesus's assurance to us that although he left, he is coming back for us. He sent his Spirit to be our comforter until he returns (John 14:26). We don't have to be troubled or afraid because he has given us peace (John 14:27).

Harden Not Your Hearts

Harden not your hearts as in the provocation,
in the day of temptation in the wilderness.

—Hebrews 3:8

What image comes to your mind when you think of "hardened hearts"? I envision something tough, calloused, thick, or impenetrable. When I researched the definition of *hardened* in my Bible study resources, I was surprised that the word was synonymous with being stubborn.

In a perfect world, there would be no such thing as a "stubborn Christian," especially when you think that the word *stubborn* characterizes someone who is unreasonably unyielding. In other words, despite all the logical arguments in the world, or despite all the evidence to the contrary, a stubborn person is not going to relinquish his or her position or belief. They are mulish! They refuse to budge, no matter what!

What lesson was the writer in Hebrews trying to get New Testament Christians to learn? Hebrews 3 (verses 8 and 15) and Hebrews 4:7 relate to the Old Testament scriptures in Psalm 95:7. This psalm is identified as a "call to worship the Lord" and is a wonderful invitation to respond to the Lord's greatness and his power. In verse 6 of this psalm, the writer beckons us to "come, worship, bow down, and kneel before the Lord our maker." Even today, Jesus is constantly calling out to us.

In Psalm 95, the psalmist writes:

> To day if you will hear his voice, harden not your heart, as in the provocation, and as in the day of temptation in the wilderness: when your fathers tempted me; proved me, and saw my work, forty years was I grieved with this generation.

What an indictment against the children of Israel. The details of those days of provoking the Lord are described in Exodus 17 (verses 1–7). The children of Israel were traveling in the wilderness, and they stopped in the place where the Lord commanded them to make their camp. However, "there was no water for the people to drink."

Have you ever been in that position before—doing what the Lord tells you to, and then feeling as if the Lord has left you high and dry? In this situation, he had. But it wasn't for their destruction! It was an opportunity for the Lord to show himself strong on their behalf (2 Chronicles 16:9). However, that wasn't good enough for them, and they were ready to stone Moses (Exodus 17:4). There are other accounts written in scripture as to how the children of Israel provoked the Lord (Exodus 15, 16, Numbers 11, and Psalm 78 are just a few). Let's just say that the Lord worked miracle after miracle on their behalf, and the previous miracles weren't enough to keep them from hardening their hearts with doubt and unbelief and being too stubborn to change.

Before I become judgmental, I want to acknowledge the many times I heard the voice of the Lord but was too stubborn to be convinced by his many acts of grace and mercy. I was more intent on doing things my way (as if I created myself). I am so thankful for that day on July 26, 1981, when I finally heard that voice and stopped being too stubborn (hardhearted) to realize that Jesus was "the way, the truth, and the life" (John 14:6). This is not to suggest that I haven't had any stubborn moments along the way! However, over the years, I have come to realize that each day is a great opportunity to hear God's voice and yield to his will for my life instead of hardening my heart!

The Desires of Thine Heart

Delight thyself also in the Lord; and he shall
give thee the desires of thine heart.

—Psalm 37:4

Receiving the desires (petitions or requests) of our hearts is a lovely promise; and it would be quite tempting to think of Jesus as our ultimate supplier, who is so willing to give us anything that we request. However, many times we fail to focus on the first part of this verse, which commands us to delight ourselves in the Lord (Psalm 37:4). God will not if we will not! The challenge for many of us is knowing the true meaning of the word *delight*.

Years ago, my curiosity regarding this word led me to research this scripture, and I discovered that the word *delight* comes from a Hebrew word that basically means "to be soft or pliable." In reading this definition,

I conjured up the image that we should be like that popular children's clay in the hands of the Lord. In other words, we should allow him to form or manipulate us any way he chooses. That is not so easy!

Oftentimes, instead of molding clay, we are like a hard clay or plaster that must be pounded, cut, or chiseled. Worse yet, sometimes the Lord must use a spiritual lubricant (our tears) to soften our hard hearts. Have you ever been in a season of life where it seemed that you cried every day? Perhaps it was the Lord sending the "rain" to soften you so that you could be pliable again. Think about how much effort you exert when you are trying to manipulate something hard. This gives us a better understanding of what the Lord experiences when trying to mold us according to his will.

How do we get ourselves to the point that we "delight in the Lord"? As I pondered this question, the Holy Spirit led me to reread Psalm 37:1–3. Interestingly, the first thing I noticed is that we need to stop fretting because of evil doers (Psalm 37:1). Moreover, we need to stop being envious of those whose work only produces more evil in the world. Finally, we need to trust in the Lord and do good things (Psalm 37:3). I wonder how many blessings would come our way if we adhered to this scriptural strategic plan.

Please do not misunderstand me! I am not suggesting

that we live our lives as monks in a monastery. God does richly give us all things to enjoy (1 Timothy 6:17). However, the scriptures also implore us to "Seek the kingdom of God first" (Matthew 6:33). As I age, I am finding out the importance of a healthy balance in my life (Proverbs 11:1; 20:23). I believe the message in Psalm 37:4 is trying to drive home the point that God is our loving heavenly Father, and he desires to bless his children (Matthew 7:7–11; Luke 11:9–13).

Psalm 37 is needful to help us understand that sometimes the evildoers and unrighteous appear to be prospering when we are not. This is painful because, as humans, we tend to measure ourselves against others instead of against God's word. When those days occur (and they will), we need to heed David's advice from this psalm. We need to realize that the evildoers will be cut off (Psalm 37:9). We also need to have the confidence that God will grant us our desires and requests (Mark 11:24; 1 John 5:15).

For Out of the Abundance of the Heart

O generation of vipers; how can ye, being evil,
speak good things? for out of the abundance
of the heart, the mouth speaks.

—Matthew 12:34

Lately, my morning prayer has been, "God, set a guard before my mouth, and keep the door of my lips" (Psalm 141:3). I find myself doing this more as I become more sensitive to how my words impact others. Additionally, I pray that I use soft answers instead of angry retorts, and positive comments instead of the negative ones. Even more, I pray that I choose words of praise instead of words of criticism. When I consider the scripture in Matthew 12:36 that lets us know that we will give an account for every idle word we speak, I realize that I need to be more careful. This takes on new meaning when I align myself with Paul's writing to the Ephesians that foolish talking should not be one of the things Christians are known for (Ephesians 5:4).

It's taken me awhile, but I'm finding it more necessary to apply James 1:19 in my life and be swift to hear and slow to speak, slow to wrath. Although our mouths may speak what is in our hearts, we still have the power to slow down and process those words and the possible effects. When we speak harsh words, the residuals can have lasting impact. No matter how profusely you apologize, sometimes the damage is irreparable.

In one of his rebukes of the Pharisees (the religious hypocrites in Jesus's day), Jesus identified the source of our words. The accounts are recorded in Matthew 12:34 and Luke 6:45, where Jesus informs the disciples that good trees bring forth good fruit, and corrupt trees bring forth corrupt fruit; for the words we speak are an overflow of what is in our hearts! In Matthew 15:18, Jesus also said, "Those things which proceed from the mouth come forth from the heart," and that is what defiles us. In other words, Jesus is letting us know that our mouths are the mirrors that reflect what is in our hearts. People cannot see our hearts, but they do hear our words!

Coming to grips with how our words impact others is one of the reasons that we need to pay close attention to the scriptures that encourage us to put off anger, wrath, malice, blasphemy, filthy communication, or corrupt communication out of our mouths (Colossians 3:8; Ephesians 4:29). Ouch! That hurts! How many times have we fallen short of this scripture! And if that scripture doesn't bring conviction, how about Ephesians 4:29, which challenges us to prevent any corrupt communication from proceeding out of our mouths. Another scripture in Ephesians 4 is v. 31, which exhorts us to "let all bitterness and wrath, and anger and clamor, and evil speaking, be put away from you, with all malice."

Jesus hears our conversations! Is he grieved by what we are saying? If we assessed our words by his word, would we pass the Philippians 4:8 test and only speak those things that are honest, pure, lovely, of good report, and which have virtue and praise? Pharisees still exist today. More often, we refer to them as hypocrites. We can identify them by what they say. What do our words say about the condition of our hearts?

Create in Me a Clean Heart

Create in me a clean heart, O God; and
renew a right spirit within me.

—Psalm 51:10

One of the many challenges I face in my quest to be identified as an exemplary teacher is establishing a classroom environment that stimulates my students to use their higher-order thinking skills. I have attended many workshops where motivating students to release their creative juices has been the topic of discussion. Inevitably, these workshops tout the "latest" research on the best practices in achieving this task.

Given the international emphasis on science and technology in the twenty-first century, it has become paramount to help students demonstrate their creativity and problem-solving capabilities. A student's ability to create is even one criteria for identifying students as "gifted."

The word *create* suggests that something new has been made. What is interesting about the word *create* is that typically we, as humans, must rely on something that is already in existence to bring into existence something new. In other words, I may have the ability to make something new, but I needed existing materials to make it. From a scriptural perspective, the unique thing about God is that when he created the heavens and the earth (Genesis 1:1), he did so without using materials that already existed.

The Hebrew word for *create* used in Genesis and many other scriptures is *bara* and it means that God brought the object or concept into being from previously nonexistent material (*Strong's Concordance*). God made something from nothing! This denotes God's sovereign power and offers further proof as to why we need him, but he doesn't need us!

In his prayer of confession and repentance, David (Psalm 51) seems appreciative of God's creative powers when he prays for God to create in him a clean heart (v. 10). David has been confronted by Nathan, the prophet, regarding his adulterous relationship with Bathsheba that led to her husband Uriah's untimely death. As David faces the truth about himself, it appears as if he realizes that there is nothing in his heart worth keeping. His request seems to acknowledge that God had to create a new heart for him.

Apparently, David realized that if his heart were simply fashioned again, he may be tempted to repeat his actions. David asked God to create in him a "clean" heart, which suggests that he wanted to be morally free from a heart that devised thoughts of adultery, murder, lying, deceit, and pride.

When we sin and come short of the glory of God (Romans 3:23), it is almost mind-boggling to believe that God can create a new situation in our lives. It might almost seem impossible when we try to reason it out with our human limitations. Let us not despair! If God did it for David, he can do it for us! God has promised that he will cleanse us from all unrighteousness if we will be like David and confess our sins (1 John 1:9). Praise God!

Wounded Hearts

He healeth the broken in heart, and
bindeth up their wounds.

—Psalm 147:3

Have you ever experienced a period of high sensitivity when, whether real or imagined, it seemed as if you were constantly getting your feelings hurt? It's almost as if someone had ripped your heart from your chest and used it for target practice in preparation for a national darts title! Those fiery darts of pain appeared to come from all directions—family members, old friends and acquaintances, colleagues, and, of course, the known enemies! If those darts just pierced your flesh, the pain would be understandable. But what is it about emotional wounds that cause an indescribable pain? Worse still, it's not a sharp pain that quickly subsides! Rather, it's a dull and intense pain that seems to permeate your entire being. At least that is how it feels to me. I try and convince myself that if I could just get to the source of pain, I could apply some medication that would soothe and heal. Unfortunately, a pill is not the cure all for a wounded heart. I am thankful that, as our master physician, God "healeth the broken in heart, and bindeth up their wounds" (Psalm 147:3).

Apparently, King David could testify about heart wounds when he wrote in Psalm 55, "My heart is sore pained within me" (v. 4). David's agony caused him to be fearful and trembling, and like most of us when faced with adversity, he wanted to flee the situation. I've been like David when he expressed his desire to have wings like a dove! For then he could fly away and be at rest (Psalm 55:6). After flying away, he would then wander off and remain in the wilderness (Psalm 55:7). David was looking for an escape. Nevertheless, because David was a man after God's own heart (1 Samuel 13:14), he knew the solution to his despair. David wrote, "I will call upon God; and the Lord shall save me. Evening, and morning, and at noon will I pray and cry aloud: and he shall hear my voice" (Psalm 55:16–17). When we suffer a heart wound, the prescription calls for continued prayer and talking to God. We can have confidence that he will respond to our needs because he is "nigh unto them that are of a broken heart" (Psalm 34:18).

Despite the assurance of eventual deliverance, sometimes the pains of heart wounds feel as if they will last forever! But we must remember that our trials and challenges are only for a season (Ecclesiastes 3:1). We may secretly pray for a life free of tears of sadness, but we must accept that while on this earth, we will have seasons of breaking down, weeping, and mourning (Ecclesiastes 3:3,4). Because of God's grace and mercy, these same scriptures comfort us and let us know that we will also experience a season of building up, laughing, and dancing. Just as the light of morning follows a dark night, we can appreciate the fact that joy will follow our season of weeping (Psalm 30:5). More important, we can rejoice because Jesus came to heal the brokenhearted (Luke 4:18). Even though we do not physically see him, we can feel his soothing presence through the comfort of the Holy Spirit (John 14:16–18). "Thanks be to God, which giveth us the victory through our Lord Jesus Christ" (1 Corinthians 15:57).

Strengthen Thine Heart

Wait on the Lord: be of good courage, and he shall strengthen thine heart: wait, I say, on the Lord.

—Psalm 27:14

I remember a time of spiritual warfare that I experienced, and the battle left me utterly exhausted. I truly felt as if I had no strength left, and I desperately needed a word from God. Inspiration from the Holy Spirit led me to read and meditate on Psalm 27. Although I had read it several times before, I was appreciative of the refreshing in my soul and spirit after reading it again. The truth of Proverbs 15:23, "A word spoken in due season, how good is it!" was apparent without a doubt, especially as I meditated on verse 14 ("Wait on the Lord: be of good courage, and he shall strengthen thine heart: wait, I say, on the Lord"). This verse seemed to be the exact scriptural prescription I needed for fixing my ailing heart. It was that word spoken at the right moment by the whisper of the Holy Spirit.

When engaged in spiritual warfare, I knew it was important to remember that "the weapons of our warfare are not carnal, but mighty through God to the pulling down of strong holds" (2 Corinthians 10:4). But I must confess that, at the time, waiting on God didn't seem like my best strategy. I just couldn't comprehend that what seemed like a simple command would be the cure! If I were to compare it to a medical analogy, it was like going to the doctor because you felt that you were about to die, and then the doctor prescribed three days of total bed rest! No potent pain pills! No miracle liquid cure! What?

As I wrestled in my mind, I was also reminded of the scriptures in Isaiah 55:8–9:

> For my thoughts are not your thoughts, neither are your ways my ways, saith the Lord. For as the heavens are higher than the earth, so are my ways higher than your ways, and my thoughts than your thoughts.

In my finite mind, it seemed as if the anxiousness of waiting would have the direct opposite effect and cause my heart more stress rather than strengthen it. Regardless of my thoughts, years of experience have taught me that God's word is "quick and powerful" (Hebrews 4:12), and so I settled myself down to prepare my wait.

While I waited, I did a deeper study on what meaning these words were really trying to convey. To my surprise, I discovered that the word *wait* implies more than just sitting and doing nothing. In my research, I found out that the Hebrew word for *wait* requires us to look forward with an expectancy and assurance. So often, I have claimed to be "waiting on the Lord," but instead, I filled my mind with negative thoughts and doubts about what God would do. No wonder I couldn't equate waiting with a strong heart. I was too busy stressing my heart, albeit unintentionally!

Without a doubt, focusing on a strong heart makes sense from a spiritual and physical point of view. I have seen firsthand the devastation a weak heart can have on the quality of life as I watched my mother suffer three heart attacks and die at age sixty-five from congestive heart failure. As I prepare to celebrate my sixtieth birthday, I am now comprehending that my mother's passing at sixty-five was way too early! I can remember all the medical recommendations she was given: stop smoking, eat healthier, exercise more, maintain her recommended weight, and eliminate as much stress in her life as possible. While my mother followed the advice of her medical providers, it wasn't enough to reverse the damage to her heart.

Now that that season of spiritual warfare is over, I am thankful to God for my testimony that I learned to wait on him. He assured me through his word that this was a time when I did "not need to fight in this battle" (2 Chronicles 20:17). I am so appreciative that "God is not a man, that he should lie" (Numbers 23:19). Isaiah 40:31 declares, "They that wait upon the Lord shall renew their strength." If his word declares that he will strengthen the hearts of those who wait on him, we can believe it and receive it!

The Meditation
of My Heart

Let the words of my mouth, and the meditation
of my heart, be acceptable In thy sight, O
Lord, my strength, and my redeemer.

—Psalm 19:14

When I was a new convert (over thirty-five years ago,),
the pastor of the church I attended would have us recite
Psalm 19:14 as our benediction. Despite the number of
years that have since passed, I still have vivid memories of
saying, "Let the words of my mouth and the meditation of
my heart, be acceptable in thy sight, O Lord, my strength,
and my redeemer."

I used to think meditations were just my thoughts.
However, I have since discovered that the Hebrew word
for *meditation* in this scripture is defined as "murmuring

sounds, a groan, or an utterance." Given that information, Psalm 19:14 has now taken on new meaning for me! Recently I pondered the question, "What does it take to make your heart utter a sound, a moan, or a groan?" Perhaps you can remember a time in your life where you have been so overwhelmed with an emotion that no words would come forth? I immediately think of a sumptuous dessert, which is so good that all I can do is mutter, "Mmm, mmm, mmm!" Words at that time are inadequate, but you immediately know that it must be very, very, very good! Perhaps this was David's experience when he penned, "O taste and see that the Lord is good" (Psalm 34:8). I firmly believe that God's desire for us is to have a heart that is so overjoyed with his word, that we can't help but utter, "Mmm, mmm, mmm," as we savor His goodness.

Through the inspiration of the Holy Spirit, David uses the previous verses in Psalm 19 as a preparatory guide in praying the prayer in verse 14. In order for us to have the meditations of our heart be acceptable to the Lord, we must realize that the "law of the Lord is perfect, converting the soul" (Psalm 19:7), so that we won't resist the changes that the Holy Spirit empowers us to make as we transition from ungodly lifestyles to a way of life that pleases him. How much simpler would our lives be if we accepted the fact that "the statutes of the Lord are right" (Psalm 19:8)!

Too often, we have the attitude that God's Word doesn't literally apply to every aspect of our lives. After all, God has given us reasoning abilities, and we can figure out some things for ourselves! Right? Not always ...

David the psalmist continues this psalm by writing that the law, the statutes, the fear, and the judgements of the Lord are "more to be desired than much fine gold," and that they are "sweeter also than the honey and the honeycomb" (Psalm 19:11). It's taken me awhile, but I am beginning to fully understand that if we don't desire God's word more than worldly pacifiers, the meditations of our heart are not going to be acceptable. God's Word is so vital that Moses wrote that "man doth not live by bread only, but by every word that proceedeth out of the mouth of the Lord" (Deuteronomy 8:3).

In addition to eating a daily diet of God's Word, if we want the meditations of our heart to be acceptable in his sight, we must hide God's Word in our heart (Psalm 119:11). "For out of the abundance of the heart, the mouth speaketh" (Matthew 12:34). Even the apostle Paul exhorted us to "let the word of Christ dwell in [us] richly" (Colossians 3:16). When all else fails, we have Paul's admonition to think only on those things that are true, honest, just, pure, lovely, of good report, and that have virtue and praise (Philippians 4:8). Surely those are the meditations that will be acceptable in God's sight!

Search My Heart

Search me, O God, and know my heart:
try me, and know my thoughts.

—Psalm 139:23

Psalm 139 acknowledges that God is omniscient (all-knowing) and omnipresent (able to be everywhere). In the first verse, David wrote that God had searched him and known him to the point that God was aware of David's downsitting and uprising. God even understood David's thoughts from afar (Psalm 139:1–2). David further wrote that there was not a word on his tongue that God didn't know about (Psalm 139:4). This type of awareness was mind-blowing to David, and he realized that it was futile to try and escape the presence of God. David posed the theoretical question, "Whither shall I go from thy spirit? Or whither shall I flee from thy presence?" (Psalm

139:7). David continued the extol God's omnipresence by sharing that there is no part of the heavens or hell that we could go and not encounter the hand of God (Psalm 139:8–10). These revelations that God knew all prompted David to praise God because David knew that he was fearfully and wonderfully made (Psalm 139:14).

As David continued writing the Psalm, he concluded that those who hated God were his enemies, and David hated them with a perfect hatred (Psalm 139:22). Interestingly, it is then that David requested that God search him and know his heart, and to try him and know his thoughts (Psalm 139:23). I have been there! I completely understand where David was coming from. When we are full of praise, it is easy to utter with our mouths endearing words to God. But what happens when God puts us to the test to really see what is in our hearts? What happens when God uses the spotlight of the Holy Spirit to search our inward parts?

Considering this thought, I remember a time when I was a new convert, full of zeal, sitting in a church service in which the pastor preached a very moving message about having our hearts in a condition in which Jesus would want to live. Afterward, he made an altar call and challenged us to ask Jesus to search our hearts and know our thoughts. I couldn't wait to rush to the altar and boldly present my request to the Lord. I wasn't there long before the Lord started revealing to me what he saw. I heard him call out hatred, variance, wrath, strife, and envy (Galatians 5:19–20). Ouch! In my spirit, I put up a hand as if to cry out, "Stop! No more searching! I can't handle the truth!"

Before the Lord finished with me, he added a few more descriptors that signified the works of the flesh, which I would rather not share. Instead of boldly walking back to my seat, I almost crawled. It took me a while to recompose myself. As I reflect on that experience, I am more thankful today for God's grace and mercy. Despite my heavy heart, I walked out of church that night with a renewed commitment to have a heart that was pleasing in the sight of God.

Several weeks later, I returned to the altar in a much more humbled state. My boldness was diminished, and in a mouselike voice, I whispered to God my love for him. Once again, I asked him to search my heart and know my thoughts. This time, I passed the test. God spoke to me that I had many of the fruits of the Spirit: love, joy, peace, longsuffering, gentleness, goodness, and faith (Galatians 5:22). I will admit that it hasn't always remained that way. However, I have never again gone to God in a bold yet self-deceptive manner, thinking that I had it altogether, as I did the night of my new-convert exuberance.

In Jeremiah 17:10, we read that the Lord said, "I the

Lord search the heart." We don't have to ask him; it's a given! However, can we trust him with the intimate areas of our lives? Sometimes we don't know what is there until the Lord sends a test to try us. David was willing to do this and ended Psalm 139 by asking that the Lord search him and see if there was anything wicked in him. If it was, David wanted it handled so that he could be led to a path that was everlasting (v. 24). That should be the goal for each of us!

When My Heart is Overwhelmed

From the end of the earth will I cry unto thee, when my heart is overwhelmed: lead me to the rock that is higher than I.

—Psalm 61:2

There are several reasons why summer has always been my favorite season. For starters, I celebrate my natural birth and spiritual rebirth in August. My wedding anniversary is also in August, which gives me another occasion to celebrate. I also love summer because the Fourth of July is my favorite holiday! What's not to love about it? Barbecues, ice cream, fireworks, beaches—to me, it has everything I love about life! I don't even have a problem with the blistering heat as I bask in the sun's golden rays. Finally, as an educator, summer symbolizes my time to be renewed after a school year of teaching. The longer I've taught, the more I have come to appreciate the opportunity to be rejuvenated.

At this point in my life, my summer of 2017 has not been one of my highlights! Even the weather has failed to cooperate with my wishes, and we have been shut in because of several rainy days. Like the sun struggling to break through the clouds, my spirit man has struggled to rejoice. It seems as if this summer, my family and I have been hit with some of everything: health concerns, several doctor visits, trips to the emergency room, a deluge of medical bills, household repair bills, broken-down cars, and failed dreams!

One morning, I just had a good old-fashioned meltdown because I couldn't find my car keys. Who would have thought that something that I had experienced hundreds of times before would be the catalyst for the floodgates of my soul to burst open! In my despair, I cried out and asked God to please help me because I didn't think that I could handle one more thing. At that very moment, I received a text from a dear friend with a message to read Psalm 61:2. Those words, "When my heart is overwhelmed, lead me to the rock that is higher than I," were sent straight from the throne room! Wow! What awesome timing. I have said it before, but it bears repeating: "A word spoken in due season, how good is it" (Proverbs 15:23). This scripture spoke to my spirit and provided the direction that I needed!

I knew that the word *heart* in Psalm 61:2 symbolized our emotions, will, or intellect. However, the definition of *overwhelmed* was not what I expected. It means "to shroud or clothe" and has a connotation that we are languishing or being covered over with darkness. In my mind, I envisioned lying flat down and being covered with layers of sheets. Each sheet seemed heavier than the one before. Before long, it's as if there were so many layers over me that I couldn't breathe! That is my visual of my heart being overwhelmed. During times like these, I could definitely identify with David's words, "My heart is sore pained within me" (Psalm 55:4). Each headache, heart ache, and disappointment of my 2017 summer had completely immobilized me. All I could do was cry (more specifically, scream out in agony).

Words penned by David in Psalm 142 perfectly described my dilemma. David wrote:

> I cried unto the Lord with my voice, with my voice unto the Lord did I make my supplication. I poured out my complaint before him; I shewed before him my trouble. When my spirit was overwhelmed within me, then thou knewest my path. (Psalm 142:1–3)

During this time of despair, I found that the rock that was higher than I was the Word of God, which is "quick and powerful" (Hebrews 4:12). I knew my problem and trusted God's Word for the solution. Psalm 55:22 encourages us to "cast thy burden upon the Lord, and he shall sustain thee, he shall never suffer the righteous to be moved." While Psalm 61:2 truly painted the state of my spirit at that time, God's words strengthened me in my time of need and once again showed me that he would not allow me to suffer beyond what I could bear (1 Corinthians 10:13). Truly, "many are the afflictions of the righteous, but the Lord delivereth him out of them all" (Psalm 34:19). On this, we can depend!

A Merry Heart

A merry heart maketh a cheerful countenance:
but by sorrow of the heart the spirit is broken.

—Proverbs 15:13

A merry heart doeth good like a medicine:
but a broken spirit drieth the bones.

—Proverbs 17:22

Proverbs 15:13 reads that "a merry heart maketh a cheerful countenance; but by sorrow of the heart the spirit is broken." As I read this scripture, I was confronted by the truth that many people of God (myself included) are sharing more testimonies of failing to experience the joy of the Lord (Nehemiah 8:10). For some, it's not a day of the doldrums here or there, but a daily battle that persists for weeks on end! In some cases, the only seeming relief has come from a prescription pill rather than the promise of Proverbs 17:22, which reads, "A merry heart doeth good like a medicine!"

Being aware of this situation for some time, in July 2014, I coordinated a fellowship service through our ladies' ministry in which we could publicly address our concerns. The theme for the program was Renewing the Mind, and it was based on Romans 12:2 where Paul exhorted the early Christians to be "transformed by the renewing of their minds." I was one of the three speakers during the evening, and my message was a discussion of suicide, anxiety, and depression in the house of God. I felt that this topic was the elephant in the room that many were too afraid to discuss. For some reason, we have perpetuated the myth that spirit-filled Christians cannot suffer from anxiety or depression, nor do they wrestle with thoughts of suicide (to which they sometimes succumb). Many Christians have voiced that they feel too ashamed or embarrassed to admit that their lives are being impaired in any capacity because of emotional distress. It's almost as if once we are born again, we should automatically become super saints—able to beat any foe or overcome every obstacle.

Since I am not a licensed professional equipped to diagnose or advise on these topics, my purpose that night was to open the door to conversation about these issues and share data and statistics about each that I had obtained from a national mental illness association. Some researchers suggest that up to 10 percent of the general population suffers from symptoms associated with depression, such as feelings of sadness, hopelessness, or restlessness; disruptive sleep patterns; loss of interest in regular activities; loss of appetite; or difficulty concentrating. Not only is the battle with depression robbing people of their joy, it is also having a major impact on their finances, both in terms of medications and prescriptions as well as lost wages!

I also wanted attendees that night to understand that mental anguish among the people of God was not a new phenomenon. As the writer of the book of Ecclesiastes wrote, "There is no new thing under the sun" (1:9). When examining the lives of well-known biblical characters, many could be described as battling depression. One example would be Hannah, who was in bitterness of soul because she could not have children. The scriptures reveal that she was so distraught that she could not eat, and all she could do was weep (1 Samuel 1:8–10). David was another biblical character who voiced dismay over his life's situations. In Psalm 77, David began his writings describing how he cried unto God, and in his day of trouble, his soul refused to be comforted, his spirit was overwhelmed, and he was troubled to the point that he couldn't even speak (v. 1–4). Even the prophet Elijah requested of the Lord that he might die (1 Kings 19:4). What is interesting about Elijah's battle is the fact that he had just prevailed in a major battle between good and evil!

Hannah, David, and Elijah emphasize the point that having the anointing and favor of God does not exempt us from feelings of anxiety or depression. Our challenge becomes what we do when those dark days come! Do we throw in the towel or do we fight the good fight of faith (1 Timothy 6:12)? I believe, as you are reading this, you will make the decision to put on the whole armor of God and prepare to do battle (Ephesians 6:11–18). As you take out the "sword of the Spirit, which is the word of God" (Ephesians 6:17), you will equip yourself with scriptures that will enable you to cut through the enemy's strongholds in your mind! When engaged in battle, remember that we do not wrestle against flesh and blood (Ephesians 6:12), so, therefore, people are not our enemies! Don't forget God's promises to never leave thee nor forsake thee (Hebrews 13:5).

David knew the key to a merry heart. In Psalm 40, he wrote that he "waited patiently for the Lord" (v.1). When we are in agony of soul and spirit, waiting for relief may seem like a most difficult task. However, David continued writing, "He brought me up also out of a horrible pit, out of the miry clay, and set my feet upon a rock" (v. 2). God put a new song in David's mouth, and it was a praise unto our God (v. 3).

Scripture References

Keep Your Heart

Proverbs 4:23

John 16:8–13

Mark 7:21–22

Genesis 6:7

Genesis 8:21

Ephesians 6:16

Lamentations 3:23

1 John 1:9

Deuteronomy 2:30

Psalm 55:4

Proverbs 28:25

Isaiah 35:4

Jeremiah 5:23

Romans 1:21

Ephesians 4:18

Thy Word Have I Hid

Psalm 119:11

Psalm 119:7

Psalm 119:2

Psalm 119:10

Psalm 119:34

Psalm 119:58

Psalm 119:145

Genesis 39:9

2 Samuel 11 (entire)

Trust in the Lord

Proverbs 3:5

Hebrews 4:12

Isaiah 55:9

2 Timothy 2:15

1 Thessalonians 5:17

Philippians 4:6–7

The Heart is Deceitful

Jeremiah 17:9

Ecclesiastes 1:9

2 Samuel 13:1–2

2 Samuel 13:3–4

2 Samuel 13:16–17

2 Samuel 13:17–19

2 Samuel 13:15

1 Kings 8:39

My Heart Is Fixed

Psalm 57:7

Acts 13:22

2 Samuel 6:14

2 Samuel 22 (entire)

1 Samuel 18:8–9

1 Samuel 24 (entire)

2 Corinthians 4:8–9

Isaiah 54:17

Troubled Heart

John 14:1

John 14:26

John 14:27

John 13:1

John 13:9

John 13:21

John 13:25

John 13:26–30

John 13:31

John 13:34–35

John 13:36

John 13:37

John 13:38

Harden Not Your Hearts

Hebrews 3:8

Hebrews 3:15

Hebrews 4:7

Psalm 95:7

Exodus 17:1–7

2 Chronicles 16:9

Exodus 17:4

Exodus 15:16

Numbers 11

Psalm 78 (entire)

Desires of the Heart

Psalm 37:4

Psalm 37:1–3

1 Timothy 6:17

Matthew 6:33

Proverbs 11:1

Proverbs 20:23

Psalm 37:9

Matthew 7:7–11

Proverbs 11:1

Proverbs 20:23

Psalm 37:9

Matthew 7:7–11

Luke 11:9–13

Mark 11:24

1 John 5:15

From the Abundance of the Heart

Matthew 12:34

Psalm 141:3

Matthew 12:36

Ephesians 5:14

James 1:19

Matthew 12:34

Matthew 15:18

Colossians 3:8

Ephesians 4:29

Ephesians 4:31

Philippians 4:8

Create in Me a Clean Heart

Psalm 51:10

Genesis 1:1

Psalm 51 (entire)

Romans 3:23

1 John 1:9

Wounded Hearts

Psalm 147:3

Psalm 55:4

Psalm 55:6

Psalm 55:7

1 Samuel 13:14

Psalm 55:16–17

Psalm 34:18

Ecclesiastes 3:1

Ecclesiastes 3:3–4

Psalm 30:5

John 14:16–18

1 Corinthians 15:57

Strengthened Heart

Psalm 27:14

Proverbs 15:23

2 Corinthians 10:4

Isaiah 55:8–9

Hebrews 4:12

2 Chronicles 20:17

Numbers 23:19

The Meditation of My Heart

Psalm 19:14

Psalm 34:8

Psalm 19:7

Psalm 19:8

Psalm 19:11

Deuteronomy 8:3

Psalm 119:11

Matthew 12:34

Colossians 3:16

Philippians 4:8

Search Me, O God, and Know My Heart

Psalm 139:23

Psalm 139:1–2

Psalm 139:4

Psalm 139:7

Psalm 139:8–10

Psalm 139:14

Psalm 139:22

Psalm 139:23

Galatians 5:19–20

Galatians 5:22

Jeremiah 17:10

Psalm 139:24

When My Heart Is Overwhelmed

Psalm 61:2

Proverbs 15:23

Psalm 55:4

Psalm 142:1–3

Hebrews 4:12

Psalm 55:22

1 Corinthians 10:13

Psalm 34:19

A Merry Heart

Proverbs 15:13

Proverbs 17:22

Nehemiah 8:10

Romans 12:2

Ecclesiastes 1:9

1 Samuel 1:8–10

Psalm 77:1–4

1 Kings 19:4

1 Timothy 6:12

Ephesians 6:11–18

Ephesians 6:17

Ephesians 6:12

Hebrews 13:5

Psalm 40:1–3

About the Author

Tanya Swygert experienced her new birth in Jesus Christ over thirty-five years ago. Since then, she has ministered God's Word throughout the United States and England.

Professionally, she has been an educator since 1998 and has been employed in various capacities at the elementary school level.

In addition to her master's degree in Early Childhood and Special Education and several educational certifications, she holds a doctorate degree in Leadership from the University of Georgia.

Married since 1978, she and her husband are proud parents of three adult children.

About the Graphic Designer

Tres Swygert, graphic designer and illustrator, designed the book cover. He has a B.F.A. degree in Graphic Design from Georgia State University. He also has a B.S. degree in Information Technology with a concentration in Digital Media. He has completed several freelance art projects.

Printed in the United States
By Bookmasters